Smart Alec's

beastly jokes

for

kids

illustrated by David Mostyn

Ward Lock Limited · London

© Ward Lock Limited 1987

First published in Great Britain in 1987
by Ward Lock Limited, 8 Clifford Street
London W1X 1RB, an Egmont Company

Typeset by Columns of Reading
Printed and bound in Great Britain
by Collins

British Library Cataloguing in Publication Data

Smart Alec's beastly jokes for kids.
  I. Alec, *Smart*
  828′.91402   PZ8.7

  ISBN 0–7063–6606–9

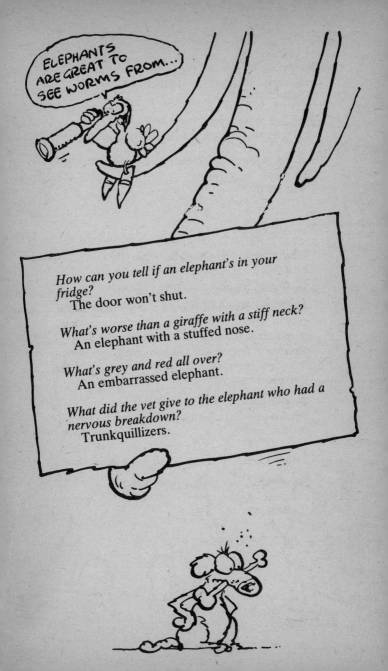

Why couldn't the two elephants go swimming?
  Because they only had one pair of trunks between them.

Why did the elephant wear brown boots?
  His black ones were at the shoe repairer!

What's as big as an elephant, but doesn't weigh anything?
  His shadow.

Why did the elephant go to the dentist?
  It had a terrible tuskache!

What should you give a seasick elephant?
  Plenty of room!

Where are elephants found?
  It's such a large animal, it's hardly ever lost.

What did Tarzan say when he saw the herd of elephants coming over the hill?
  'Here come the herd of elephants over the hill.'

Why did Noah name the big animal an elephant?
  Because it looked more like an elephant than any other animal.

Why do elephants float down the river on their backs?
So they won't get their toes wet?

Why do elephants wear pink tennis shoes?
Because white ones get dirty too fast.

Why do elephants have wrinkled knees?
It's from playing too many games of marbles.

How can you tell an elephant from a grape?
A grape is purple.

ONLY KNOWN DEFINITIVE DRAWING OF THE PIRANUS BITEYERHANDOFFIMUS.

Why are elephants coloured grey?
    So you can tell them apart from canaries.

What looks like an elephant and flies?
    A flying elephant!

What looks like an elephant, flies, and is very dangerous?
    An elephant with a machine gun.

How do you know if an elephant's in your bed?
    By the big 'E' printed on his pyjamas.

BEEN HAD

NOT A SAUSAGE!

How can you tell there's an elephant under your bed?
   Your nose is touching the ceiling.

Where do elephants come from?
   Great big storks!

Define willpower.
   'An elephant eating only one peanut.'

Some people think of an elephant as an animal with a vacuum cleaner on its face!

Other people think of it as a mouse that's taken vitamin pills and has worked out with weights!

Here's some good advice — if you grab an elephant by the hind legs and he tries to run away, it's best to let him go!

'What's the difference between an elephant and an egg?'
   'If you don't know I'm certainly not going to send you shopping!'

IF YOU WANT TO SEE
SIDNEY SNAKE EAT
JOGGER JIM — FLICK
THROUGH THE PAGES
STARTING AT THE
BACK →

What does an elephant do if it breaks a toe?
  Gives up ballet dancing.

What's the best way to attract an elephant?
  Make a noise like a peanut.

Cross an elephant with a mouse and what do you get?
  Giant holes in the skirting board!

How much did the psychiatrist charge to see an elephant?
  £550. Fifty pounds for the visit and £500 for a new sofa.

How does an elephant get up a tree?
  He sits on an acorn and waits for it to grow.

'Are peanuts fattening?'
   'Have you ever seen a skinny elephant?'

*How would you get five elephants into a
Volkswagen?*
   Simple — two in front, two in back and one
   in the glove compartment.

'Why are elephants wrinkled all over?
   'Did you ever try to iron one?'

*How would you make a hamburger for an
elephant?*
   First, you get a very big roll . . .

Why did the elephant lie in the middle of the road?
   He enjoyed tripping ants.

What has big ears and hops?
   An elephant on a pogo stick.

Why do elephants wear sandals?
   To stop themselves sinking into the sand.

'Foul,' said the referee when the elephant stepped on the mouse during a football match.
   'I'm sorry,' said the elephant, 'I only meant to trip him.'

Did you hear about the elephant who went to the beach to see something new in trunks?

'I wish I had enough money to buy an elephant.'
   'What do you want with an elephant?'
   'Nothing — I just wish I had that much money!'

Why wasn't the elephant allowed on the plane?
   His trunk was too big to fit under the seat.

DON'T WORRY JUST A FEW MORE TO GO!

BURP

Why does an elephant have a trunk?
Because he doesn't have a glove compartment.

What goes clomp, clomp, clomp, squish — clomp, clomp, clomp, squish?
An elephant with one wet sneaker.

I know one kid who thinks that elephants have trunks because they have no pockets!

What do you get it you cross a worm wth an elephant?
Gigantic holes in your garden.

I CAN'T COMPETE WITH THAT!

Why does it take an elephant longer to pack for a trip than a rooster?
    Because an elephant has a trunk to pack —
    a rooster simply carries a comb.

'What's the difference between an elephant
and a mattababy?'
    'What's a mattababy?'
    'Nothing — what's the matter with you?'

Woman: Do you make life-size enlargements
    of photos?
Chemist: Certainly.
Woman: Good — here's a photo of an
    elephant!

HORRID NIF!

BURP

What did Thomas Edison Elephant invent?
 The electric peanut!

'My sister's got a memory like an elephant.'
 'And a shape to match!'

Give me an example of nonsense.
 An elephant hanging over a cliff with his
 tail wrapped around a daisy!

*What might you get if you crossed elephants
with locusts?*
 I'm not sure, but if they ever swarm —
 watch out!

Patient: Can a man be in love with an elephant?

Doctor: No.

Patient: In that case do you know anyone who wants to buy a very large engagement ring?

Boy elephant to girl elephant, 'And if we ever marry who knows — one day we may hear the *thunder* of little feet.'

What do you get if you cross an elephant with a boy scout?
   An elephant that helps little old ladies across the street.

Why do elephants have trunks?
   So they have somewhere to hide when they see a mouse!

BURP

There's one kid who thinks that a mouse is an elephant that's gone on a diet!

'Why do elephants paint their toenails red?'
  'So they can hide in a strawberry patch.'
  'I don't believe that.'
  'Have you ever seen an elephant in a strawberry patch.'
  'No.'
  'See — it works!'

What do you get if you cross an elephant and a cactus?
  The biggest porcupine in the world!

How can you disguise an elephant?
  Make him wear a moustache with dark glasses.

Elephant: You're the puniest creature I've ever seen.
Mouse: I can't help it — I've been sick.

Son: Can I feed a peanut to the elephant?
Father: Give him two — business has been good this week.

Why did the elephants go on strike?
  They were tired of working for peanuts.

How do you get down from an elephant?
  You don't. You get down from a swan.

Would you rather an elephant attacked you, or a gorilla?
  I'd rather he attacked the gorilla.

Have you ever heard of a baby raised on elephant's milk?
Yes, a baby elephant.

Why has an elephant got a trunk?
To keep his tennis rackets in.

How do you stop a herd of elephants charging at you?
Make a trunk call, and reverse the charge.

A theatre usher was astonished to see a big elephant sitting in an aisle seat munching on a bag of peanuts.
'Hey,' he whispered, 'where did you get the peanuts? I thought the machine was busted.'

Judge: You were arrested for stealing an elephant. Why did you do that?
Defendant: My father once told me, 'Son, if you're going to steal, steal big!'

Why do elephants wear dark glasses?
If you had all these stupid jokes told about you, you wouldn't want to be recognised either!

What's worse than an elephant on water skis?
A porcupine on a rubber life raft.

What's black, likes peanuts, and weighs two tons?
 A chocolate-covered elephant.

Man: How much do you sell elephants for?
Trainer: 50p.
Man: Wow, that's cheap — 50p an elephant?
Trainer: No — 50p a pound.

Why do elephants paint their toes red, blue, green yellow and pink?
 So they can hide in the jelly bean jar.

Why didn't the travelling elephant tip the bellboy when he checked into the hotel?
 Because the bellboy didn't carry the elephant's trunk to his room.

What is big and green and has a trunk?
   An unripe elephant.

'My daddy's got a leading position in the circus.'
   'What does he do?'
   'He leads the elephants.'

What's the biggest ant of all?
   The eleph-ANT.

What do you get when you cross a parrot with an elephant?
An animal that tells what it remembers!

What weighs two tons, has tusks and loves pepperoni pizza?
An Italian elephant.

How do you catch an elephant?
First you buy a fishing pole and put a peanut on the hook . . .

What weighs two tons and has red spots?
An elephant with measles.

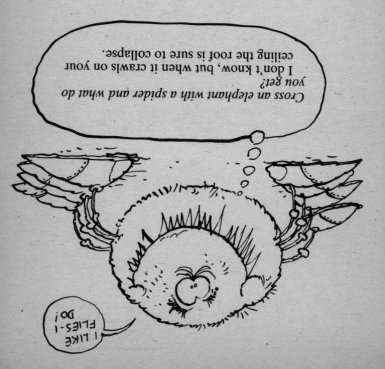

Cross an elephant with a spider and what do you get?
I don't know, but when it crawls on your ceiling the roof is sure to collapse.

I LIKE FLIES—I DO!

What's the difference between an elephant and a chicken?
    An elephant can get chicken pox, but a chicken can't get elephant pox!

What's the difference between a tiny elephant and a gigantic mouse?
    About 2,000 pounds!

What time is it when an elephant climbs into your bed?
    Time to get a new bed!

What's worse than an elephant with a sore nose?
A turtle with claustrophobia!

How can you tell if there's an elephant in your sandwich?
When it's too heavy to lift off the plate!

How do you tell the difference between an elephant and a gooseberry?
Elephants don't grow on bushes.

What's the difference between an elephant and a jar of peanut butter?
An elephant doesn't stick to the roof of your mouth!

What did the grape say when an elephant stepped on it?
Nothing — it just let out a little whine.

Why does an elephant wear ripple-soled shoes?
To give the ants a 50-50 chance.

How do you make an elephant float?
With a glass of milk, a scoop of ice cream, and an elephant.

How did the duck get flat feet?
By teaching a clumsy elephant how to dance!

What's the best way to stop an elephant from charging?
Take away his credit cards!

What's the best way to tell an elephant with a short temper that he's fired?
Call him long distance!

What's grey, has two wheels and weighs two tons?
An elephant on a motorcycle.

'My mum is so gentle, she wouldn't hurt an elephant.'

What did the keeper see when the elephant squirted water from his trunk?
A jumbo jet!

Cat — the one animal that never cries over spilt milk.

Did you know that London has the highest number of cats *purr* capita?

As soon as the cat saw a mouse, he make a feline for it.

I'm learning to break into homes — a cat burglar is teaching MEOW.

Where do Arab cats come from?
   The PURRsian Gulf.

Cross a Chinese cat with an alley cat and you'll wind up with a Peking Tom.

Name the famous cat composer.
   PUSSINI.

Did you hear about the African cat that escaped from the zoo?
   He made the *headlions*!

I'm sorry that I yelled at my cat — I hurt her *felines*.

Did you hear about the leopard who is so clean, he keeps himself spotless?

Where do cats go when they die?
To PURRgatory.

One stray cat met another stray cat.
'Meow' purred the first.
'Bow-wow' answered the second.
'What kind of reply is that? Have you lost your mind?'
'Not at all,' was the proud reply. 'I've just become interested in foreign languages.'

A man got out of bed in the middle of the night to go to the toilet and accidently stepped on his cat's paws. As the cat let out a yowl, the man shouted at her defensively, 'Who tells you to go around barefoot?'

My wife kept bothering me to buy her a car — she wanted a Jaguar. I finally got her one — that night it ate her up.

'Why's your cat so small?'
    'He was brought up on condensed milk.'

Show me a cat that just ate a lemon and I'll show you a sourpuss.

What do you call a crazy chicken?
    A cuckoo cluck.

Cross Satan with a chicken and what do you get?
    Devilled eggs!

CHICKIN JOKES

Cross a chicken with a turkey and what do you get?

A churkey!

Cross a chicken with a bell and what do you get?

An alarm cluck.

If a chicken crosses the road, rolls in the mud and comes back, what is it?

A dirty double crosser.

Cross a chef and a rooster and what do you get?

A cook-a-doodle-doo.

'My dog thinks he's a chicken.'
'Take him to a vet.'
'I can't — we need the eggs.'

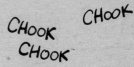

What do you call a greasy chicken?
A slick chick.

Chicken farming is a *fowl* operation.

When chicken broth was first canned,
everyone thought it was *souper*!

When's the best time to buy chicks?
    When they're going cheep.

Cross a hen with a cement mixer and what do you get?
    A brick layer.

'I want to buy a chicken.'
    'Do you want a pullet?'
    'No — I'll carry it home in my bag.'

Why did the farmer call his chicken, Robinson?
    Because it crew-so.

Cross a chicken with a coyote and you'll get an animal that crows at the moon!

Who cracks jokes about chickens?
    Comedihens!

Why did the chicken sit on the axe?
    So she could hatch-et.

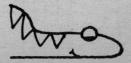

There's one rooster who's the laziest animal on the farm. At daybreak he waits for the other roosters to crow, then he simply nods his head.

'Gosh, the meat of this chicken sure is tough.'
    'It must have been a really bad egg in its youth.'

First farmer: Why do you keep your hens in hot water?
Second farmer: It's an experiment to see if they'll lay hard-boiled eggs!

First man: That restaurant serves chicken that really tickles your palate.
Second man: What do they do?
First man: They leave the feathers on!

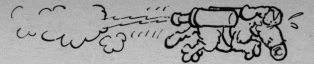

Which is less intelligent — a large chicken or a small chicken?
The large chicken — it's a bigger cluck!

Customer: There's no chicken in this chicken soup.
Waiter: And you won't find a horse in the horseradish, either!

Why are rooster feathers always smooth and neat?
Because a rooster always carries a comb.

Name the famous building built by chickens.
The Henpire State Building.

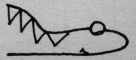

When does a chicken get all red?
When it's henbarrassed.

What book tells you all about chicken?
The Hencyclopedia.

The mother chicken was so happy — her son was going to be a *hengineer*.

What do you call a smart chicken?
   A hentellectual.

Where should you take a sick horse?
   To the Horsepital.

What's the hardest thing about learning to ride a horse?
   The ground!

One father told his errant son, 'I'd horsewhip you if I had a horse!'

I rode a well-mannered horse — whenever we came to jump a fence he let me go first!

Horseshoes — an outdoor pitching game where the first rule is to remove the horse.

It's a wise horse that knows its own fodder.

Stable — a horse house.

Tongue Twister: Say the following words ten times as fast as possible — *Horse House*.

When a horse gets to the bottom of its nosebag, I guess it's the last straw.

Horse — an animal that more people bet on than get on.

Think about it — horsepower was much safer when only horses had it.

It's strange, but a horse eats best when it doesn't have a bit in its mouth.

A fat person who takes up horseback riding to reduce weight quickly takes several pounds off — the horse!

I know a teenager who just got a job at the horse stables. He's complaining that his work is piling up!

I know one horse that was really clever. During a race he was nose to nose with another horse, so in order to win he stuck out his tongue!

Some people think of a horse as a sure-footed animal — when it kicks it doesn't miss!

Other people think of a horse as ill-mannered. After all, it always sleeps with its shoes on!

Many a horse feels a bit down in the mouth.

Why's a horse a terrible dancer?
   It has two left feet!

The night before he went to the races, dad kept dreaming of number 6. He felt it was an angel sending him a message. So, the next day he went to the racetrack and in the sixth race he bet all his money on horse number six. It came in sixth!

If you want all your troubles off your mind, go horseback riding.

Ivan: You can tell the age of a horse by the teeth.
Andrea: But who wants to bite a horse?

Did you hear about the idiot who lost £500 betting on a horse? He lost £200 on the race and £300 pounds on the instant replay!

Two morons bought a horse each and intended to keep them in the same field.

'How can we tell which horse is which?' asked the first moron.

'I'll tie a red ribbon to my horse's tail,' said his friend.

'But the ribbon might fall off and we'll be faced with the same problem.'

'Okay,' suggested the friend, 'In that case, you have the black horse and I'll take the white one.'

Doctor: Ever have an accident?
Patient: No.
Doctor: You never had an accident in your entire life?
Patient: Well, last spring I was out riding my horse and it tossed me over the fence.
Doctor: Don't you call that an accident?
Patient: No — I'm sure the horse did it on purpose!

First jockey: I had some trouble with my horse this morning. He wanted to go one way and I wanted to go the other way.
Second jockey: How did you settle it?
First jockey: The horse tossed me for it.

Parrot — a wordie birdie!

*Cross a parrot with a centipede and what do
you get?*
  A walkie talkie!

Crow — a bird that never complains without
caws!

What do you call a crazy crow?
  A raven maniac!

First farmer: Is that scarecrow any good?
Second Farmer: I'll say — it's given the crows
    such a fright they've brought back the seed
    they stole *last* week!

What did the blackbird say to the scarecrow?
  'I can knock the stuffin' out of you!'

Why did the sparrow fly into the library?
  It was looking for bookworms.

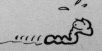

What do you call an intellectual owl?
  Birdbrain.

What is the best advice to give to a worm?
  Sleep late!

What do you get when you cross an owl with an oyster?
  A bird that drops pearls of wisdom!

An owl picked up the telephone and asked, 'Whooo is it?'

What bird was a famous American lawman?
  Wild Bill Peacock.

There's a wonderful children's book about peacocks — it contains some beautiful *tails*!

Which birds are religious?
    Birds of prey.

Frank: My teacher does bird imitations.
Harry: Really:
Frank: Yeah — she watches me like a hawk!

Did you hear about the young pigeon that was
spanked for using fowl language?

Boy: Did you hear about the crazy scientist
    who crossed a lion with a parrot?
Girl: What did he get?
Boy: Nobody knows, but when it talks — you
    listen!

How did the chicken farmer get up in the morning?
    He had an alarm cluck!

Farmer's wife: I've made the chicken soup, dear.
Farmer: Good — I was afraid it might be for me!

Teacher: Name a bird that doesn't build its own nest.
Student: The cuckoo.
Teacher: Very good. How do you know?
Student: Simple — everyone knows the cuckoo lives in a clock!

Naughty Nancy threw a rock,
Hit the cuckoo in the clock.
Mother couldn't hear a tick,
Nancy claimed, 'The bird is sick!'

What happened to the newly-hatched egg?
It chickened out!

A hungry pelican caught a large fish and said,
'This sure fits the bill!'

Did you hear about the seagull that landed on
a harbour buoy? It was a case of *buoy meets
gull*!

There's one parrot who's really spoilt. Every
time its wealthy owner comes home, the bird
says, 'Polly want a cracker — with *caviar* on
it!'

What does a 1,000 lb parrot say?
  Polly want a cracker — NOW!

One bird was so sick it had to go to the hospital for special *tweetment*!

My sister sings like a bird — a *vulture*!

What do you get if you cross a chicken with a guitar?
  A hen that makes music when you pluck it!

Science Teacher: Can anyone name a bird that's become extinct?
Student: My canary — the cat made her extinct two days ago!

'Do you know what we got when we crossed a parrot, a hyena, and the writer of this book?'
  'No — what?'
  'A special bird that laughs at its own jokes!'

Cross a woodpecker with a parrot and what do you get?
  A bird that talks to you in Morse Code!

'Why don't people like to hear stories about woodpeckers?'
   'Because they're *boring*!'

Why did the hens complain?
   They were sick of working for chicken feed!

One hen even tried to run away — she was tired of being all *cooped* up!

A father owl told his son, 'It's not *what* you know that counts — it's *whooo* you know!'

One book company publishes detective stories as well as books about owls. You might say they specialize in *whooo-done-its*.

What kind of birds are found in Portugal?
    Portu-geese!

What do geese get when they're cold?
    Goose pimples!

What's green and pecks at trees?
    Woody Woodpickle!

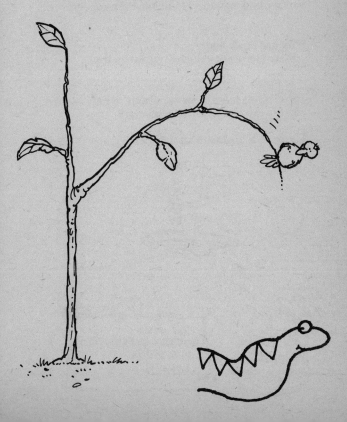

Why do birds in a park like to talk to Chinese people?
  Because they sometimes speak pigeon English!

What do you call a gathering of hundreds of pigeons?
  A bird herd!

'Where do birds invest their money?'
  'In the *stork* market!'

Little Sandra stared for a long time at the stork in the zoo, then turned at last to her mother and signed, 'He never even recognized me!'

Why are birds poor?
  Because money doesn't grow on trees.

Birds don't have to worry about money — two can always live as *cheeply* as one!

Duck — a bird with snowshoes!

BOTTY CREAM

FOR SORE BOTTIES EVERYWHERE ONE DIP IS ENUFF

Duckling — a bird that grows down while it grows up!

Why did the turkey cross the road?
   To prove he wasn't chicken!

Where do stinging insects look for information?
   In the encycloBEEdia.

Name the famous insect artist.
   Pablo BEEcasso.

How does a stinging insect feel when it's just lost a loved one?
   BEEreaved.

Adult stinging insects always remind their children 'Don't misBEEhave!'

What's the favourite movie of bees?
   The Sting!

Where do wealthy bees go to live?
   In suburBEEa.

Put a bee in a honey pot and to him it's utopBEEa.

How do stinging insects taste?
    BEElicious!

I know one stinging insect who's into health foods. He's a macroBEEotic cook!

Name the famous bee who wrote children's books.
    BEEatrix Potter.

When stinging insects can speak two languages equally well, they are known as BEElingual.

What Middle Eastern country has the most stinging insects?
    Saudi AraBEEa.

What disease killed thousands of stinging insects?
    The BEEbonic Plague.

Where do you take a sick bee?
    To the hospBEEtal.

A bee that's all washed up and has passed his peak in power is known as a has BEEn.

A bee that has given away state secrets is a BEEtrayer.

What warning is given to all bees beefore they set out to find fields of flowers?
    BEEware.

What might a father do to his son (of-a-bee) if he's been naughty?
    BEEt him!

If a bee doesn't understand something, what might it say?
    'This is BEEyond me!'

A bee that gives in to authority is?
    oBEEdient.

What might a bee say as a statement of surprise?
    'Well, I'll BEE!'

What do we call a bee who doesn't take care of his BEElongings properly?
   SlopBEE.

A bee that acts as a messenger or peacemaker is called a goBEEtween.

Name the kind of candy that bees just love.
   Jelly BEEns.

Name the favourite cartoon character of bees.
   SnoopBEE.

What classic composer do bees prefer to listen to?
    BEEthoven.

A bee that wears his hair long and listens to 'cool' music is a hipBEE (or BEEtnik).

Where is the favourite resort to which bees go during their vacation?
    Miami BEEch.

Nervous bees are said to have the heBEEgeBEEs.

What rock group do bees prefer to listen to?
The BEEtles.

Name their favourite tune (written, of course, by the BEEtles).
'Let it BEE'.

What do we call an unassuming and unpretentious bumblebee?
A humbleBEE.

A wild headlong flight of frightened bees is known as a stampBEEde.

A bee who feels deeply in love with his wife usually refers to her as a honey(BEE).

What do we call a bee who is about to get married?
    BEEtrothed.

A bee's favourite sport is rugBEE.

What do all bees shout when their rugBEE team scores?
    yipBEE!

You too can learn to prepare delicious bee food if you simply buy a special book of reciBEES.

Which flowers do bees like to plant?
    BEEgonias.

Name the undercover agency in which some bees work?

The F. BEE I.

Bees that are circus performers, acrobats or gymnasts, sometimes practice on a trapBEES.

A bee who's feeling happy and content is hapBEE.

A bee who's in a bad mood is usually very grumpBEE.

Name the broadcasting system in England to which bees listen on the radio.
    The BEE BEE C.

Where are bees that have been born prematurely usually kept?
    In an incuBEEtor.

If a bee gets bitten by a sick dog, he could get raBEEs.

What precious stones do bees use in making jewelry?
   ruBEEs.

When a bee gets tired, he becomes sleepBEE.

A bee who can address a large audience and hold their attention can be called an especially good sBEEker.

Where are bees housed?
  In an aBEEary.

A bee who can pilot a plane is an aBEEator.

Bees prefer to have their food cooked on a
barBEEcue.

Their favourite hound dog is a BEEgle.

A bee that has a firm conviciton in something
is a true BEEliever.

The scientific study of the life processes of bees is called BEEology.

If a bee acts strangely, we say he is BEEzar.

What do we call the special fairs set up to collect money to help out bees in need?
    BEEzaars.

The pulse of a bee comes from his heartBEEt.

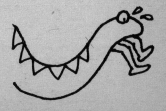

A bee who cheats in school by looking at another student's paper is a copBEEcat.

What do all mother bees have to tell their children before sending them off to school?
 BEEhave!

Bees who drink too much nectar could get an overamount of sugar in their blood, possibly leading to that dreaded disease diaBEEtes.

Collecting stamps to most bees is a hobBEE

Young bees just love to ride on a hobBEE Horse.

What do bees like to eat for breakfast?
 BEEcon and eggs.

Everything a bee owns is known as his BEElongings.

A bee who's puzzled and confused is BEEfuddled.

What do you say to a bee if you want it to go away?
    BEEgone!

A bee that wants to become a father will BEEget children.

I MEAN – WHAT DO BEES DO? APART FROM MAKING STUPID OLD HONEY

What do we call bees who are so down and out that they have to ask for food and shelter?
  BEEgars.

If a young bee comes home late, father might ask, 'Where have you BEEn!

Name the favourite alcoholic beverage of bees.
  BEEr.

What do we call those bees who are born with 100 legs?
  centiBEEdes.

A bee that's sentenced to death will be executed by being BEEheaded.

What do we call a bee's backside?
  His BEEhind.

Bees who return from the dead are called?
  ZomBEES.

A bee that overdrinks by sipping too much sweet nectar may become?
    oBEEse.

What do we call a bee who can use both its arms equally well?
    amBEEdextrous.

A bee who can live on both land and water is?
    amphiBEEous.

A newborn bee is called a baBEE.

A bee that's called upon to watch a young bee while his parents buzz out for the evening is known as a baBEEsitter.

What do we call a bee who wins a prizefight?
A champBEEon.

Bees who live in the Phillipine Islands are called?
FiliBEEnos, what else?

What do we call the recorded history of a bee's life?
His BEEography.

A bee who drives a taxi for a living is a cabBEE.

Name the famous story about a giant white bee.
   MoBEE Dick.

What one question do hordes of bees discuss among themselves concerning life and death?
   'To BEE or not to BEE?'

The favourite toy of bees is a frizzBEE.

Bees enjoy doing a Latin dance known as the
BEEguine.

Milking a cow is *udder* joy.

What's the favourite astrological sign of cows?
  Taurus (what else?)

When a male cow meets a female it's a case of
bull meets girl.

WE APOLOGISE
FOR THE LACK OF
CHUCKLES ON THESE PAGES
BUT SOMEONE MIGHT FIND THEM
FUNNY!

What do you get if you cross an octopus with a cow?
    An animal that can milk itself.

What do cows watch on TV?
    The moos of the day.

What happens to cows during an earthquake?
They give milk shakes.

What's the easiest way to count a large herd of cattle?

Use a cowculator.

Where do American cows go for a holiday?
  To sunny Cowlifornia.

Why did the candy factory hire the farmer's daughter?
  They needed someone to milk chocolates.

If two cows helped each other what would that be?
  COWoperation.

What do you get from a forgetful cow?
  Milk of amnesia.

Where do cows go for entertainment?
To the mooovies.

What kind of cattle are always broke?
Bum steers.

Why don't cows ever have any money?
Because farmers milk them dry.

What music do bulls like best?
Cow-lypso music.

What would you call it if the cow that jumped over the moon fought Taurus the Bull?
  Steer Wars!

'What's cowhide used for?'
  'To keep the cow together.'

A man walked into a pub one day with a calf under his arm. 'Where on earth did you get that thing?' asked the bartender.
  'I won him in a raffle,' mooed the cow!

TWEEK

Does a cow with hiccups churn its own butter?

There's an old saying among cows: NO MOOS IS GOOD MOOS.

Cross a cow with a duck and what do you get? An animal that gives milk and quackers.

Milking cows is easy — any jerk can do it!

Some people think of a tin of beef as an armoured cow!

Teacher: How does one gain good posture?
Country boy: Keep the cows off and let it grow awhile.

What state in the United Staes has lots of cows?
  MOO York.

What is the favourite game of cows?
  MOOsical chairs.

Where might you see a prehistoric cow?
  In a mooseum.

Dad just bought a cow to eat the grass in our garden. He's a sort of lawn mooer!

What did the bull say to the cow?
  When I fall in love it will be for heifer.

Why do cows go to sunny beaches?
  To tan their hides!

Why did the cowboy break his nose at the rodeo?
    They gave him a bum steer!

He was *beefing* about it for a long time.

Production costs can be very high in the diary business — a lot of expenses are in curd.

What happened to the farmer who milked 50 cows in one day?
    He had to go to a doctor to get his fingers straightened!

Cross a cow with a porcupine and what do you get?

A steak with a built-in toothpick.

There are four kinds of milk — sweet milk, sour milk, buttermilk and condensed milk. This explains why dairy cows are equipped with four taps!

There once was a girl named Tina
who milked a cow with a vacuum cleaner.
The farmer grumbled and gave her the sack
so Tina turned the cow over, and put the milk
back!

Did you know about the summer of '46 when it was so hot that cows were giving *evaporated* milk?

'Why do you feed your cows money?'
'It's an experiment to see if they'll give rich milk!'

When the first branding iron was invented the cattle were really *impressed*!

Look at a cow and remember that the greatest scientists have never discovered how to turn grass into milk!

One old bull told a cow, 'You're only as young as you *veal*.'

A millionaire dairy farmer told his friend, 'All I have I owe to udders.'

The price of milk has become so high that one woman decided to buy a cow — and take things into her own hands!

What's the difference between a cow and a baby?
A cow drinks water and makes milk; A baby drinks milk and makes water.

Why do cows wear bells?
  Because their horns don't work.

Why shouldn't you cry if a cow falls over a cliff?
    There's no use cryin' over spilt milk!

What cow speaks Russian?
  Ma's cow!

Cross a cow with a mule and what do you get?
  Milk that has a real kick to it!

What happened to the man who stole the milk?
He was taken into custardy!

Why did the butcher put the dairy cow on a scale?
He wanted to see how much the milky weighed!

Did you hear about the matador who took judo lessons to learn how to throw the bull?

The price of milk has become so high that one farmer thinks it's cheaper to buy ice cream and melt it down!

What's the difference between an angry audience and a cow with laryngitis?
One boos madly, while the other moos badly.

Since the farmer found a *whey* to make money, he's doing much *butter*.

What do you get if you cross a Tyrannosaurus rex with a cow?
A monster that eats anyone who tries to milk it.

Roy: I know a male steer that's nine feet tall and weighs 10,000 pounds.
Joy: That's a lot of bull!

What kind of cows live in the far north?
Eskimoos.

An Englishman, a Scotsman and a German were walking through a field when they spotted a cow.

Englishman: Look, there's an English cow.

German: No, No — it must be a German cow.

Scotsman: You're both wrong — it's a Scottish cow — look underneath — it's got bagpipes!

A man went to see a bullfight in Spain and kept bragging, 'I bet I can lick that bull.'

The bull tossed him for it and the man came down heads!

Wife: I need a new leather coat.

Husband: But the one you have is only two years old.

Wife: Yes — but it was second-hand. Remember that the cow wore it for five years before me!

Cow — one of the few animals with a built-in fly swatter.

Mamma cow was introducing her calf to the ways of the world when they were suddenly confronted by a wild fox. Mamma immediately began barking like a fierce dog. The fox took off. Turning back to her calf, Mamma announced, '*That* shows the importance of learning a second language.'

There's trouble on the dairy farms — workers are pulling for higher prices.

Visitor: What does that painting represent?
Artist: That is a cow grazing in a pasture.
Visitor: Where is the grass?
Artist: The cow has eaten it.
Visitor: But where is the cow?
Artist: You don't suppose she'd be fool
  enough to stay there after she'd eaten all
  the grass, do you? She went off to another
  pasture.

Little Ivan had never been to a farm before.
  Now, visiting his aunt's farm, he gazed
  curiously at a cow.
  'What's that?' he asked.
  'That's my cow,' said his aunt.
  'And what are those things on her head?'
  'Horns,' replied his aunt.
  Just then, the cow mooed long and loud.
  Ivan was startled. 'Which horn did she
  blow?'

A ferocious lion killed and ate a bull.
  Afterwards he felt so happy he roared and
  roared. A hunter heard him roar and shot
  him.
  Moral: When you're full of bull, you'd
  better keep your mouth shut!

A speeding car ran over one of Farmer Brown's cows.

'Don't worry,' said the driver of the car. 'I'll replace your cow.'

'Really?' said the farmer. 'Are you able to give milk?'

A city boy stood and watched the farmer milk the only cow he had. The next morning the farmer was furious because the cow had been stolen during the night.

Farmer: Drat the thief that stole our cow!

City boy: I wouldn't worry about it they can't get too far. After all, you drained her crankcase last night.

A city girl was visiting a farm with her class. She kept watching a cow chewing her cud and finally asked the fearmer, 'Doesn't it cost you a lot to keep giving that cow chewing gum?'

As the farmer said when he put the new pail underneath the cow, 'One good *urn deserves an udder*!'

Cream is more expensive than milk because the farmers have to work harder to get the cows to sit on smaller bottles!

What happens to cows when they die?
    They're cream-ated.

Some people think of a cow as an animal that lays milk.

'Flash —. it's just been reported that a woman was killed taking a milk bath. The cow slipped and fell on her head!'

'Doctor, doctor — please help me. I think I'm a cow.'
   'How long has this been going on?'
   'Ever since I was a calf.'

City girl: What's that animal over there?
Farm boy: A Jersey cow.
City girl: How can you be certain when it has no licence plates?

Mack: Hey Butch, where'd you get that dumb dog?
Butch: Dumb — nothing. Why this morning he got up and brought in the cows. Then he took them back out to pasture. Next, he came back, separated the milk and loaded it on the truck to take to the creamery.
Mack: Gosh, did he make the butter too?
Butch: What do you mean, make the butter? Who ever heard of a dog doing *that*?

What do you call the boss of a dairy?
    The big cheese!

First cow: Why the sour look on your face?
Second cow: My milk has spoiled!

Teacher: Where do you get milk from?
Pupil: The milkman!

Sign in a restaurant:

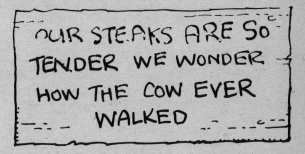

OUR STEAKS ARE SO
TENDER WE WONDER
HOW THE COW EVER
WALKED

Farmer to cow, 'You're looking much *butter*, Elsie!'

'I can't decide whether to buy a bicycle or a cow for my farm.'
'Won't you look silly riding a cow?'
'I'd look even sillier trying to milk a bicycle.'

A woman decided that she wanted to take a milk bath so she asked the milkman for 25 gallons of milk.
'Do you want it pasteurised?' asked the milkman.
'That won't be necessary,' replied the woman. 'Up to my knees will be fine.'

'What a strange-looking cow,' said the young girl from the big city. 'Why doesn't she have horns?'
'Well,' answered the farmer, 'some cows are born without horns, some shed their horns, some are dehorned, while some breeds don't have horns at all. So you see, there are lots of reasons why cows might not have horns but the reason why *that* particular animal hasn't got horns is because she isn't a cow — she's a horse!'

What did the city boy say when he saw a pile of old milk bottles in the farmer's field?
'Hey, look at that cow's nest!'

WARBLE

If you sing to a cow, do it in the key of *beef-flat*.

Written on a dairy truck:
FROM MOO TO YOU IN AN HOUR OR TWO.

What bulls make famous swordsmen?
The Three MOOscateers.

'There's a lot of money to be made in the cattle industry.'
'So I've *herd*.'

Cow to farmer, 'Go ahead and milk me — see if I give a *dram*.'

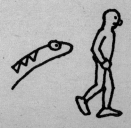

Mother cow to calf, 'Everything I tell you seems to go in one ear and out the udder!'

Did you hear about the sick male cow who had a bully-ache?

And one male cow is very special — he's *doubull*-jointed.

'Is it true that grass is good for the eyesight?'
'Must be — I've never seen a cow wearing glasses.'

One idiot farmer put up a sign:
WARNING TO COWS — KEEP OFF
THE GRASS!

'How do you keep milk from turning sour?'
'Leave it in the cow!'

*What do you call a male cow who bets on
horse races?*
A gambuller.

What male cow is the head of the police?
The Chief Constabull.

Male cows that join the navy are *Abull*-bodied
seamen.

What do you call a sleeping cow?
A bulldozer.

Cow to bull, 'Stop *steering* at me!'

Man: How do you milk a caterpillar?
Farmer: First, you get a very low stool!

'How do you know if an animal is a cow?'
'You can detect the faint odour of grass on
its breath.'

Farmer to friend: 'I've been experimenting
with my cow, brushing her teeth every
morning. Now she's giving dental cream.'

The Sunday School teacher was talking to her class of ten year olds when she suddenly asked: 'Now, why do you think the Children of Israel made a Golden Calf?'

The children were silent until one spotty little boy put up his hand and said: 'Please Miss, perhaps it was because they didn't have enough gold to make a cow.'

What do you call religious cows?
True Bullievers.

Where do cattle eat?
In a COWfeteria.

Calfs love to ride on a *cowrousel*.

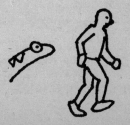

A male cow that comes from the upper classes is a member of the Nobullity.

What kind of cows eat other cows?
  Cannibulls.

What do cows wear if they don't want to be seen?
  Camooflage.

What famous member of the bovine family discovered America?
  Christopher COWlumbus.

What other bovine is a famous Western outlaw?
  Bully the Kid.

Isn't it strange — a black cow eats green grass and gives white milk which makes yellow butter!

All these jokes about cows have been *udderly* ridiculous!

An ant that walks in his sleep is a *somnANTbulist*.

Why did the lobster get a divorce?
  It discovered it was married to a crab!

What do you give a bald rabbit?
  A harepiece!

Why should you never steal a pig?
  It might squeal to the police!

Who snatched the baby octopus and held it to ransom?
  Squidnappers!

What did the dying pup say?
  'Well, I'll be doggone!'

What do you call a camel with three humps?
  Humphrey!

What do porcupines eat with their cheese?
  Prickled onions!

Which two types of fish do you need to make a shoe?
  Sole and 'eel.

What would you do with a sick wasp?
  Take it to a waspital!

Why did the lobster blush?
  He saw the salad dressing!

What did the drunken chicken lay?
  Scotch eggs!

What do you call a crate of ducks?
  A box of quackers!

Many other ants are famous sciANTists.

Ants that live in Cairo are *EgyptiANTS*.

Name the most famous female Egyptiant?
   CleopANTra.

What kind of ants study stars?
   Antstronomers.

Name the most famous sciANTist of them all?
  Albert ANTstein.

Who was the famous Chinese ant that had so many famous sayings?
  CANTfucious.

If an ant is going to have a baby she goes to an *ObstetriciANT*.

An ant that treats sick animals is a *veterianariANT*.

Some ants that join the military become parANTroopers.

One ant can't stop herself from stealing. She's a KelptomANTiac.

Another ant loves to start fires. He's a pyromANTiac.

What's the weakest part of an ant?
  Its ANTchilles heel.

A western ant might be a rANTcher.

Female ants often join the FemANTist movement.

There's a monster known as the Abominable SnowANT.

What giant ant is now extinct?
 TyrANTosaurus rex.

Really naughty ants have their heads chopped
off by a guillANTine.

The first Russian ants into outer space were
called CosmonANTS.

What ant first sailed round the world?
 FerdinANT MagellANT.

Name the famous French ant.
   NapoleANT

Ants with two heads are known as
SiANTmese twins.

Beware, or SatANt will have his way!

Ants that preach the gospel are evANTgelists.

Watch out — here comes FrANTkenstein!

A sick ant could be rushed to hospital and placed in ANTensive care!

Dead ants are buried in a cemANTery.

To find ant more about ants read the ANTcyclopedia.

Donald had been seeing a psychiatrist for over a year because he thought he was a basset hound. He met a friend one day who asked, 'How's your treatment coming along?'

'I'm not cured yet,' said Donald, 'but at least I've stopped chasing cars.'

A psychiatrist was exmaining a new patient.

'How many ears does a dog have?' he asked.

'Two,' answered the patient.

'How many eyes does a dog have?'

'Two.'

'And how many legs does it have?'

'Gee, Doc,' remarked the patient, 'haven't you ever seen a dog?'

The man finally had a nervous breakdown and thought he was a dog. He ate dog food for supper, slept curled at the head of the bed, and even barked when he heard noises in the night. His wife was a very sympathetic woman, and took him to a renowned psychiatrist who promised he could help. After six months of therapy the man seemed to return to normal. He ate at the table, watched television, and was able to carry on a rational conversation without starting to bark. The psychiatrist decided it was time to end the therapy. The man was overjoyed.

'I just know I'm okay now,' he told the doctor. 'Feel how cool my nose is.'

Yesterday, I spent all evening trying to pull
the teeth of our neighbour's dog.
Unfortunately, they were too far embedded in
my thigh.

Doctor: Don't you know that my hours are
only from 2-4 p.m.?
Patient: Yes, I do. But I'm afraid the dog that
bit me didn't.'

Teacher: The composition you wrote on the
topic '*My Dog*' is exactly like your
brother's.'
Student: I know. It's the same dog.'

'Can a Dalmation change its spots?' asked the
teacher.
 All the children said 'No,' except one little
girl.
 'Yes it can,' she said. 'I have a Dalmatian,
and whenever he gets tired of one spot, he
simply gets up and moves to another.'

DON'T GO ANY FURTHER -
THIS IS THE GOOD
BIT!

The teacher explained, 'Quite a number of plants and flowers have the prefix "dog". The dogrose is only one, but there are many more.' She asked, 'Who can name another?'

'I can,' shouted a student. 'Collie-flower.'

Doctor: I'm sorry to have to tell you this, but the dog that bit you has rabies.

Patient: Please give me a pencil and paper.

Doctor: Are you thinking of writing your will now?

Patient: Of course not. I'm going to make a list of all the people I want to bite.

Husband: Darling, I don't think you'll ever teach that dog to obey you.

Wife: Nonsense, my dear. Don't you recall how obstinate you were when we first married?

'She calls her husband and her dog by the same pet name.'

'Doesn't that cause confusion from time to time?'

'No — not at all. She always speaks gently to the dog.'

Some people are so unlucky — I know a man who owns a St Bernard, a German Shepherd, and an Irish Setter. Still, the only one who barks at him is his wife!

An irate customer entered a pet shop and told the owner, 'You promised me that the dog you sold me was good for rats, but three months have passed and he hasn't caught even one.'

'So?' asked the owner. 'Isn't that good for rats.'

Another annoyed customer burst into the same shop about an hour later complaining, 'That dog I bought here is almost blind.'

'Well,' replied the owner, 'remember I told you she was a friendly, lovable and devoted creature, but that she didn't look good.'

Before closing the pet shop the owner received one last complaint. He had sold a giant watchdog to a woman who moved into a new house. She phoned and said, 'Last night burglars broke into my house and stole a fortune in jewels while the watchdog you sold me slept.'

He told her, 'What you should do now, madam, is come and buy a little dog to wake up the big dog.'

A sign displayed in the window of a pet shop reads:

WE HAVE A WARM HEART FOR
COLD NOSES.

'Doctor, doctor, my dog is becoming very neurotic — can you help him?'

'Unfortunately, no.'

'Why not? You're supposed to be the leading German psychiatrist in the field of animal behaviour.'

'Because I vill not allow a dog on ze couch!'

Mrs Handel dropped by to pay her new neighbour a visit. They were sitting and having a chat over a cup of coffee when suddenly a dog trotted into the room and asked, 'Have you seen the Sunday Times?' The owner placed the paper in the dog's mouth and she trotted back out of the room leaving Mrs Handel totally flabbergasted. 'You mean your dog can actually read the newspaper?' gulped the woman. 'No, no, no,' said the owner. 'Don't be fooled. She only looks at the comics.'

An old lady went to purchase enough wool to knit her dog a sweater.

'How big is he?' asked the woman behind the counter.

'That's a little difficult to describe,' replied the old lady.

'If you bring the dog in, I'll be able to judge the amount of wool you'll need,' suggested the sales person.

'Oh, I couldn't do that,' exclaimed the old lady. 'It's supposed to be a surprise for him.'

A television director heard music in the street, and saw an old man with a dog and a horse. While the dog played accordian and the horse sang, the old man collected coins from people passing by. The director was so impressed that he offered the three a job for 500 dollars a week on his new television show. When the day came to perform, however, they never showed up at the television studio. The director later found the three on the same street playing for passersby.

'What on earth is wrong with you?' he asked the old man. 'You could be earning 500 dollars a week, but instead you're playing for nickels and dimes in the street.'

'My conscience is bothering me,' answered the old man. 'I don't think it's fair to fool the millions of people who'd be watching your show.'

'What do you mean?' asked the director.

'The truth is,' said the old man, 'that the horse can't sing a note. The dog's a ventriloquist.'

A puppy's best friend is its mutter.

Puppies without parents are usually sent to an arfanage.

The people who train puppies tend to be dogmatic.

A puppy's training is intensive, and as far as I can tell, its life is mostly ruff.

Sometimes a young dog will get laryngitis, in which case he'll feel totally yelpless.

Trainers may give their young dogs a treat and let them watch their favourite cartoon character — *Pupeye* the Sailor.

A postman rushed to the emergency room of a nearby hospital shouting that a dog had bitten him on his leg.

'Did you put anything on it?' asked one of the nurses.

'No,' replied the postman. 'He seemed to like it just as it was.'

'Teacher,' shouted Ivan, the class comic, 'my dog knows arithmetic.'

'That's amazing!'

'Yeah,' said Ivan, 'just ask him how much twelve take away twelve is and he'll say nothin'.'

Another wit, Andrea, who was in the same class said, 'Why my dog even knows his own name.'

'What's his name?' asked the teacher.

'Woof!' replied the girl.

Not to be outdone, Ivan told the teacher, 'On Sunday I took my dog fishin'.'

'Did you have any luck?' the teacher wanted to know.

'Afraid not,' said Ivan, 'Next Sunday I'm going back to usin' worms.'

As giggles filled the classroom, Andrea said, 'Yesterday my dog fell from a tree that was over 100 feet tall.'

'Was she hurt?' asked the teacher worriedly.

'Not really,' said Andrea. 'She only climbed up about two feet.'

A young by walked into a pet shop and asked if there were any dogs going cheap. The wiseguy salesman said, 'Sorry, kid, all our dogs go woof.'

The young boy asked the same salesman, 'My dog keeps chasing everyone on a bicycle. What can I do?' 'Try taking away his bicycle,' advised the salesman.

A woman took her hound into a restaurant, sat down at a table and began to read the menu. A waiter remarked, 'I've never seen a dog sitting on a chair in our restaurant.'

'And you'll never see another one,' said the hound. 'Not at these prices.'

Another inmate at the same asylum kept complaining that he swallowed a mad dog.

'It's stuck in my intestines, tearing my guts apart,' he moaned. This continued for six months until one day the inmate had an acute attack of appendicitis. The surgeon at the institute had to operate, and he decided that this was a supreme opportunity to effect two cures at one time. He sent for a little brown spaniel, and when the patient woke up from his operation, the doctor showed him the animal. 'There — you'll be perfectly okay now — look what we found.' The inmate grabbed his stomach in panic and shouted, 'You've got the wrong dog — the one I swalled was white with black spots!'

'My dog is sick. Can you recommend a good animal doctor?'

'Sorry — all the doctors I know are people.'

The little boy was spending the weekend with his grandmother. He came running in from the backyard yelling, 'Nanny, nanny, there's a gigantic dog as big as a truck in the neighbour's yard.'

'Bobby,' said the grandmother, 'haven't I told you a hundred billion times not to exaggerate?'

What small dog is particularly dangerous?
A chihuahua with a machine gun.

'Doctor, doctor, my dog just swallowed a
large bottle of aspirins. What should I do?
'Try to give him a big headache.'

What do you get if you cross a Doberman with a werewolf?
  A very nervous postman.

Cross a lion with a bulldog and what do you get?
  I'm not sure but if goes 'Arf', you'd better listen!

If you cross a man-eating tiger with a dog, you'll wind up with an animal that eats people then buries their bones.

'Bruce,' screamed the shocked mother, 'you mustn't pull the dog's tail.'
  'I'm not pullin' the dog's tail,' said Bruce, 'I'm standing on it and he's doin' all the pullin'.'

I saw a movie the other day showing how bloodhounds were trained to work with police. The film was a dogumentary.

'Look at the dog I got for my girlfriend.'
　'Wow, you're lucky. How'd you ever make a trade like that?'

Joan: I've lost my precious little dog.
Jane: Why not put an advertisement in the newspaper under LOST AND FOUND?
Joan: The poor little creature can't read.

In another incident, a very thin man had to stop playing 'fetch the stick' with his Great Dane. More often than not, the dog brought *him* back.

Little girl: What kind of dog is that?
Little boy: It's a police dog.
Little girl: It doesn't look like a police dog.
Little boy: That's because it's an undercover agent.

Joel: Why is it that every time the doorbell rings your dog moves into a corner?
Richard: It's because he's a boxer.
Joel: Well it can't be a very good one — just look at his face!

There's a dog I know who just loves to be scrubbed four times a day. His owner is not absolutely certain of his breed, but he thinks it's a shampoodle.

'Tom,' shouted Mrs Thorndike to her little boy, 'keep that dog out of this house — it's full of fleas.'

'Stay out of the house, doggie,' said the youngster, 'it's full of fleas.'

Little girl: I would like to buy a puppy. How much are they?
Salesman: Twenty pounds apiece.
Little girl: But I want a *whole* puppy.

A little boy of five saw a small dog whose tail had been cut off, leaving only a short stub. He asked his mother, 'Did the dog's tail get broke off, or did they drive it in?'

The next week the same little boy, when he saw a snake for the first time yelled, 'Come quick! Here's a tail wagging without a dog!'

'Got anything to cure fleas on my dog?'
  'Maybe — what's wrong with the fleas?'

Hector: It's a strange thing — all dogs
   regardless of how vicious they may be, will
   come and lick my hand.
Katy: Perhaps if you ate with a knife and fork,
   instead of with your fingers, they wouldn't
   be so friendly.

If a dog's prayers were answered, it would
rain bones.

Ivan: Every morning my friend took his dog to school, until the day came when they had to part.
Andrea: Why?
Ivan: The dog graduated.

Shirley and her friend, Rhonda, met one day for lunch.

'I entered my dog in a special contest, and I won first prize,' said Shirley.

'That's fantastic!' beamed Rhonda.

'I guess so,' remarked Shirley, 'but I wanted the dog to win.'

Believe it or not, one Texas oilman was so rich he actually bought a boy for his dog.

Dog show: Oodles of poodles.

What's the difference between a gorilla and a banana?
Have you ever tried peeling a gorilla?

He: What's the difference between a monkey and a banana?
She: I don't know.
He: Well — I'll never trust you to buy bananas!

How can you tell an ape from a grape?
A grape is red!

Patient: I keep seeing giant apes with long hairy arms.
Doctor: Have you ever seen a psychiatrist?
Patient: No — just giant apes with long hairy arms!

What did the sensible monkey say to the crazy monkey when he gave him his dinner?
   'Your nuts.' (You're nuts.)

What would you get if you crossed King Kong with a chicken?
   The biggest cluck in town!

What ape fries potatoes in the zoo?
   A chip monk!

What's the best way to attract a monkey in the jungle?
   Make a noise like a banana!

What do you call an ape that drinks ten cups of hot chocolate a day?
  A cocoa-nut!

What's yellow and smells of bananas?
  Monkey puke!

What ape was a famous American pioneer?
  Daniel Baboone.

What ape was the first emperor of France?
  Napolean Baboonaparte.

DISCREET COFF

Boy: My father is a vet for a zoo.
Girl: Really — how does he treat a giant gorilla?
Boy: With the utmost respect!

How can you tell if a monkey's been sleeping in your bed?
Look for banaka skins under the covers!

When is a shop's delivery van like a monkey?
When it travels from branch to branch.

What kind of apes talk a lot?
Blab-boons.

How do you measure the height of a gorilla?
  With a t-ape measure.

First orangutang: What on earth is that thing
  over there?
Second orangutang: That's a hippopotamus.
First orangutang: Fancy having to live with an
  ugly face like that!

A gorilla went into a pub and ordered a coca
cola. The bartender, trying to take advantage
of the ape, said, 'That will be two pounds,
please.' Then the bartender added, 'We don't
get many gorillas coming in here.'
  'No wonder,' replied the gorilla, 'at two
pounds for a coca cola!'

*How do you know if a gorilla's been in your
fridge?*
  There'll probably be hairs on the butter!

Godzilla: I think I'll eat up the city of Hong Kong. Would you care to join me for dinner?

King Kong: No thanks — I don't really like Chinese food.

A man was standing in Piccadilly Circus with a box of gorilla powder in his hands. He was spreading it all over the street when a policeman walked up to him.

Policeman: Why are you spreading gorilla powder all over?

Man: To keep the gorillas away.

Policeman: But there are no gorillas in this area.

Man: See how well it works!

There's a new book which has just been published called *Ten Years in a Monkey House* by Bab Boone.

Cross a chimpanzee with a jackass and what do you get?
    A monkeydonkey!

First hunter: I just met an enormous gorilla in the jungle.
Second hunter: Did you give him both barrels?
First hunter: Both barrels? I gave him the whole gun!

What did the chimp say when he heard his sister had just given birth?
    Well — I'll be a monkey's uncle!

Which monkeys are Irish?
    O'rangutangs!

What's big and hairy, and flies at over 1,000 miles an hour?
King Kong-corde!

What do you do when a gorilla has a blocked nose?
Run like crazy if he sneezes!

What would a female gorilla wear in the kitchen?
An *ape*-ron!

What did the man say when he saw King Kong with dark glasses?
Nothing — he didn't recognize him!

What ape is like a citrus fruit?
An orange-utang!

How can you tell when a monkey is drunk?
From the smell of nuts on its breath.

Why are gorillas big and hairy?
So you won't mistake them for strawberries!

Why was the gorilla rushed to the hospital?
He had *ape*-pendicitis!

Did you hear about the scientist who crossed a cat with a gorilla? He got an animal that puts *him* out at night!

Did you hear about the scientist who crossed a parrot with a gorilla? The new animal grabbed the scientist by the throat and asked, 'Who's a pretty boy?'

The gorilla at the zoo was pregnant, and all the workers were making bets on what the sex of the infant would be. On the day of the delivery the vet announced, 'It's a *girl*illa!'

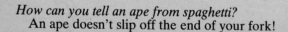

How can you tell an ape from spaghetti?
    An ape doesn't slip off the end of your fork!

Where does a ten-ton gorilla sleep?
Anywhere it wants!

Cross a kangaroo with a gorilla and what might you get?
Giant holes all over Australia!

Did you hear about the chimp that went in for yoga and finished up as a monkey puzzle!

How do gorillas show they like a performer?
With loud *ape*-plause!

Ivan: Did you hear about the formal dance in the zoo?

Fred: No — what happened?

Ivan: The penguins came in tuxedoes and the monkeys wore their tails!

What's the best way to persuade King Kong to sit up and beg?
Wave a 1,000 pound banana in front of his nose!

What's the difference between a flea and an ape?
An ape can have fleas, but a flea can't have apes!

'Why did King Kong join the army?'
'He wanted to learn about *gorilla* warfare.'

'What tree can a gorilla hold in its hand?'
'A *palm* tree.'

What's the difference between a gorilla and a kangaroo?
About 3,000 miles!

How can you tell a gorilla from a banana?
Try to pick it up. If you can't, it's either a gorilla or a very heavy banana!

YES – YOU GUESSED – IT'S ME IN A FAKE GORILLA HEAD

What looks like an ape, flies, and is very dangerous?
A flying gorilla with a machine gun!

Teacher: Why do gorillas have hairy coats?
Student: Because they'd look silly in a plastic mac!

What do you call a happy ape?
A *gayrilla*!

Why is a gorilla large, hairy, and dark?
Because if it was small, round and white it would be an aspirin!

What female sheep tells funny stories?
A EWEmorist (humourist).

Cross a sheep with a llama and what do you get?
   A little llambaaa.

What do you call miniature sheep?
   LillipEWEtians.

Thieves sometimes steal sheep and hold them for ramsom (ransom).

The famous Chinese sheep villain is *Fewe Manchu*.

Lambs born prematurely are usually placed in an *incEWEbator*.

Sheep on the run from the law are *fEWEgitives*.

What sheep fought at the battle of Jericho?
   JoshEWEa.

When sheep die they have a *fEWEneral*.

Young wayward lambs are called jEWEvenile delinquents.

Which side of a sheep has the most wool?
   The outside.

What song do sheep sing?
   'Oh, I've got plenty of mutton . . .'

As one ewe said to the ram, 'Don't you try to pull the wool over my eyes!'

Where do sheep go for haircuts?
To the baaa baaa shop.

All sheep are required to read about the
adventures of *EWElysses* (Ulysses).

There's one female sheep who can't do
anything right — she's simply *EWEsless!*
(useless)

'Doctor, doctor, I've just swallowed a sheep.'
   'How do you feel?'
   'Very baaad!'

One idiot farmer fed his sheep iron pills
hoping they would grow steel wool!

To err is human, to shear — ovine.

The sheep were crammed into the building.
They stood wool-to-wool.

It was a hot summer, and the shepherd found
himself in the middle of a *bleat* wave!

SHEEP DON'T
HALF MAKE
EWE SWEAT

Do sheep who find it hard to sleep count people?

Farmer's motto:
SHEAR AND SHEAR ALIKE

Cross a porcupine with a sheep and you wind up with an animal that knits its own sweaters!

What's the favourite store of sheep?
  Woolworth's — where else?

What did the male sheep sing to the female sheep?
  I Love EWE . . .

Cross a gnu with a sheep and you'll wind up with a new ewe — or would it be a gnuewe?

Science teacher: The fleas we find on common pets are small and dark-coloured.
Pupil: I always thought they were white.
Teacher: Where did you get that idea?
Pupil: Once I heard a poem that went, 'Mary had a little lamb — with fleece as white as snow.'

How many female sheep escape the farm?
  Very fewe.

When a sheep dies the farmer will deliver a
fitting EWElogy.

Remember Mary who used to take her lamb
to school? Well she's grown up and still takes
her lamb to school — only now it's between
two slices of bread!

A female monster sheep is called *Dracewela*.

A male monster sheep is a *Rampire*.

Their offspring will be?
   Lambpires!

Why do white sheep eat more than black sheep?
   Because there are so many more of them!

Name the sheep statue that stands in New York Harbour.
   The StatEWE of Liberty.

What sheep is strong enough to hold up the world?
    HercEWEles.

When a female sheep is really happy it bleats out — EWErika!

A ram might open the door for his lady and say, 'After Ewe.'

At Christmas, sheep get together and sing Ewele Tide Carols.

Sheep that eat in a restaurant first ask to look at the *MenEWE*.

When sheep join the armed forces, they have to wear a EWEniform.

Why do sheep sweat?
    It's usually because of high EWEmidity.

When sheep have pimples on their face, it shows they're going through pEWEberty.

Some sheep try to act like people — they want to be EWEman beings.

Some day we may have a popEWElation explosion!

'Now, Jimmy,' said the teacher, 'a little bird told me that you're starting to swear.'

'It must have been one of those *damned* sparrows!' replied Jimmy.

I just heard a sad but true story of a turtle who fell in love with a German helmet.

Take a lesson from the turtle — he doesn't make any progress until he sticks his neck out.

Fishing — a jerk at one end of the line waiting for a jerk at the other end!

It's a crime to catch a fish in some lakes, and a miracle in others.

Fishing trip — a reel treat.

Finding a worm in your apple is not so bad as finding only half a worm.

What good does it do the worm to turn — he's the same on all sides.

QUICK- THEY'RE PLAYING OUR JOKES

A wise worm turns in before the early bird turns out.

A visitor from South Africa was telling his Texan host about the size and fierceness of the mosquitos in Africa. Then he remarked, 'I see you don't bother to screen your windows here in Texas.'

'No,' replied the host, 'we simply use mousetraps!'

Frog — a pygmy kangaroo.

A frog is the only thing that has more lives than a cat — it croaks every night.

Show me a frog on a lily pad, and I'll show you a toad stool.

A young conceited lion stopped some passing animals and asked, 'Who's the king of the jungle?'

'You are, O mighty one,' said the antelope.

'None but you,' replied the chimpanzee.

'Who else but you?' answered the zebra.

Finally the lion approached an irritable old elephant who reacted to the question by grabbing the lion and hurling him 50 feet away. The lion picked himself up, brushed himself off and moaned, 'Okay, okay — don't lose your temper just because you don't know the answer!'

The parrot is a creature that does a lot of talking even when it has nothing to say.

In the kingdom of the birds, the parrot is the best talker — and the worst flier.

Rattlesnake — a tattle tail.

What do you call a snake that works for the government?
A civil serpent.

What did the two lice do when they moved to a new address?
They gave their friends a louse-warming party.

I just heard about a snake charmer who married an undertaker. They now have towels marked, '*HISS*' and '*HEARSE*'.

Once upon a time there were three bears:
Papa Bear, Mama Bear, and Cammembert.

George S. Kaufman

Never pat a bear until it's a rug.

The rooster isn't unpopular because he gets
up early — it's because he has so much to say
about it.

Patience is a virtue, but it will never help a
rooster lay an egg.

If you cut off a chicken's head, you increase
its activity but not its longevity.

Nowadays the riddle is not why does the chicken cross the road, but how?

Giraffe — the highest form of animal life.

A giraffe has to eat an early breakfast if it wants the food to reach his stomach by lunch!

Giraffes are not good at apologizing — it takes them a long time to swallow their pride.

Skunk — a community scenter.

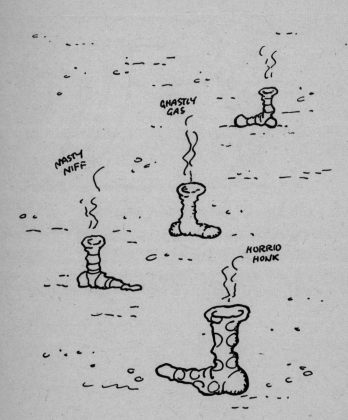

You can lead a skunk to water, but you can't
force him to stink!

Pity the defenceless skunk whose spray pump is out of odour.

I know a man who was accused of being the cruellest man in the village. Right after he bought a homing pigeon he moved house!

Zebra — a horse behind bars.

I just heard about an Irishman who named his pet zebra 'Spot!'

What happens to illegally parked frogs?
   They get toad away.

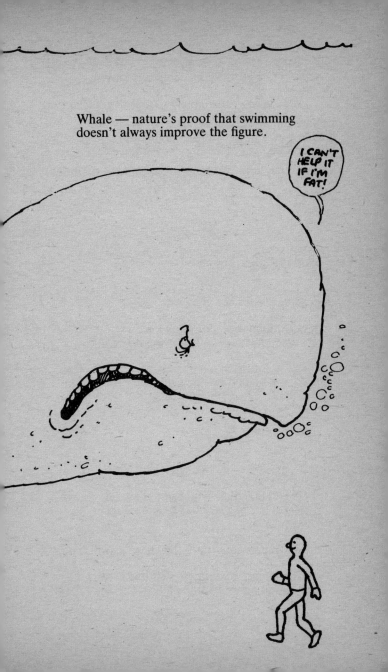

Take a lesson from the whale — he never gets into trouble until he comes up to spout.

Kangaroo — the largest species of grasshopper known to man.

To a kangaroo, every year is leap year!

Mama firefly said proudly, 'Isn't my son bright for his age?'

One lightning bug to another: 'Got to glow now!'

The habits of skunks are phew!

Many a girl who marries for mink later discovers that what she really got was a skunk.

The American tourist can always be recognised at a bullfight — he's the one who cheers the bull!

Kangaroo — a pogo stick with a paunch.

The only female who can tell everything she has in her bag without looking is a lady kangaroo.

When pigs eat dinner they have a swill time.

The reason a young pigs eats so much is because he wants to be a hog.

Farmers feel that higher prices for pork has created a gold mine in the sty.

Here's a bit of practical advice — in baiting a mousetrap with cheese, always leave room for the mouse.

Did you hear about the entomologist who crossed moths with glowworms? He produced moths that could find their way around dark closets!

Did you hear about the beautiful but hungry Greek termite who lunched a thousand ships?

When termites want to relax do they take a coffee table break?

An ill-informed father was showing his kids around the Natural History Museum. They arrived at an exhibit of a stuffed ostrich.
Father: This is the ostrich — now extinct.
Son: But dad, the ostrich isn't extinct.
Father: Well, *this* one is!

Did you hear about the turkey farmer who installed a gobblestone driveway?

They say an elephant never forgets — but what's he got to remember?

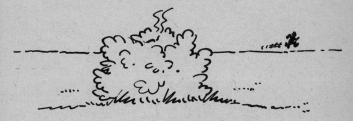

A skunk in the bush is worth two in the hand.

Nobody can behave like a skunk without someone getting wind of it.

Skunks are disliked because they put on such awful airs.

Mosquito — another creature that doesn't get a slap on the back until it starts to work.

Two goats were roaming the pasture when they found an old discarded reel of film. As they proceeded to eat the celluloid, one goat said, 'Good, don't you think?'
    'Oh, I don't know,' replied the other goat, 'I think the book was much better.'

Did you hear about the panda who tried to mate with a harmonium? Experts fear it may create a pandamonium!

You can always tell when the mosquito season is here. People start using four-letter words like OUCH!

A dolphin asked his playful mate, 'Did you do that on porpoise?'

Do unto otters as you would have them do unto you.

The quizzical expression of the monkey at the zoo comes from his wondering whether he is his brother's keeper or his keeper's brother.

Leopard — a dotted lion.

How do you start a race of fireflies?
  Ready, set, glow!

Mermaid — a deep she fish.

Did you hear the story about the two weevils?
One worked hard and got ahead in life. The
other didn't and remained the lesser of two
weevils.

Did you hear about the African chef who
boiled a hyena and made himself a laughing
stock?

Moose — a horse with TV antenna.

Camel — an animal with a face that launched a thousand quips.

Which came first — the caterpillar or the butterfly?

Lamb is sheep at any price, but venison is always deer.

Did you hear about the intellectual donkey?
  He was a real smart ass!

A man stood beside his donkey and started singing, 'I get a kick out of you . . .'

What's a cheerful hippopotamus called?
  A happypotamus!

What do you call a hippopotamus with long hair?
  A hippie-potamus!

What was the hippopotamus doing on the highway?
    About two miles an hour.

What animal with two humps is found at the North Pole?
    A lost camel.

What did the baby porcupine say to the cactus?
    'Is that you, mama?'

What do you get when you cross a porcupine with a goat?
    A kid that's hard to handle!

What's a frog's favourite flower?
A croakus.

Where do frogs fly their flags?
On the tad pole.

What's white outside, green inside and hops?
A frog sandwich.

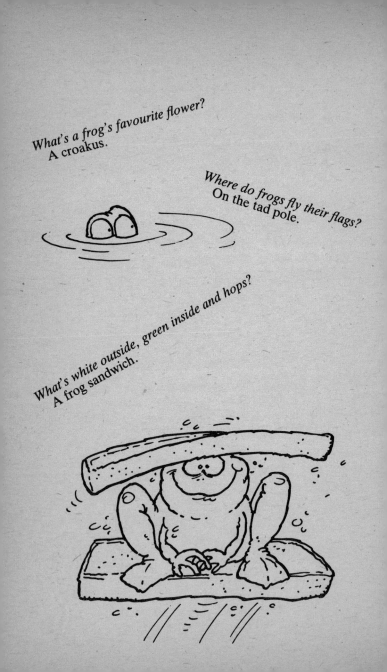

What happens when a frog's van breaks down?
It gets toad away.

What is green and goes dit dit dot dot?
A morse toad.

Two frogs got married and lived hoppily ever after.

What do frogs order for lunch?
Croakettes.

What do you get if you cross a man with a goat?
    Someone who butts into other people's affairs.

Of many a shepherd it's been said
Whenever he's lonely, he'll just goat to bed.

What did the beaver say to the tree?
    It's been nice gnawing you.

The mama beaver told her child, 'A good beaver is never *stumped*.'

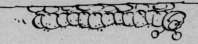

What is worse than a centipede with corns?
A hippopotamus with chapped lips.

What did the hungry donkey say when it only had thistles to eat?
  'Thistle have to do.'

Two mice moved house, invited their friends and had a *mouse-warming* party.

What's the difference between a coyote and a flea?
  One howls on the prairie, while the other prowls on the hairy.

What branch of the armed forces did the werewolf join?
  The Hair Force.

When rabbits join the armed forces, they go into the HARE FORCE.

'Is this river good for fish?'
  'Must be — I can't get any of them to leave!'

Did you hear about the jelly fish?
 It set!

What do you get when you cross a cocoa bean with an elk?
 Chocolate moose.

Why do giraffes have long necks?
 To connect their heads to their bodies.

What did the grizzly take on holiday?
 All the bear essentials.

Lucy: Is it correct to say that you water your horse?
Mother: Yes.
Lucy: Then I'm going out to milk the cat.

Paddy: I've just bought a pig.
Sam: Where are you going to keep it?
Paddy: Under my bed.
Sam: What about the smell?
Paddy: Oh, it won't mind that.

First fly: How's the new baby?
Second fly: Very restless — I had to walk the ceiling all night with her.

What type of snake is good at sums?
 An adder.

What happened to the adder with a cold?
 She adder vipe her nose!

Why should you never say anything to a rattlesnake?
 Because it's a tattletail.

What did the python say to its victim?
 'I've got a crush on you.'

What's Hissing Sid's favourite football team?
  Slitherpool.

First tiger: I don't feel well.
Second tiger: It must have been someone you
  ate!

Where do hogs keep their money?
  In piggy banks!

*How do you find out where a flea has bitten
you?*
  Start from scratch.

What goes 'croak, croak' when it's misty?
  A froghorn.

What do reindeer say before they tell a joke?
  This one will sleigh you!

Why do skunks argue?
  Because they like to make a stink!

What do you give a pig with sore skin?
  Special oinkment.

What did the croaking frog say to his friend?
  I think I've got a person in my throat!

What would you get if you crossed a flea with a rabbit?
  A bug's bunny.

Jack: If your dog was chewing your favourite book what would you do?
Jill: I'd take the words right out of his mouth.

How does an octopus go into battle?
  Well armed!

Mother python is worried about her daughter who is eighteen today, and never had a crush on anyone!

Who has more fun when you tickle a mule?
  He may like it, but you'll certainly get a bigger kick out of it!

Why do chickens watch TV?
  For hentertainment.

Name the animal that talks the most.
  A yak — it's always yakking!

From a medical point of view pigs are unique. After all, first you kill them, then you cure them.

The male centipede said to the female, 'You sure have a lovely pair of legs, pair of legs, pair of legs . . .'

A male octopus married a female and together they walked down the aisle arm-in-arm-in-arm-in-arm-in-arm . . .

'Do moths cry?'
　'Yes — haven't you ever seen a mothbawl?'

When is a car like a frog?
　When it's being toad.

Meow — a catty remark!

A goose is a bird that grows down before it grows up!

What do you call a neurotic octopus:
A crazy mixed-up squid.

What do you call a cheerful kangaroo?
A hoptimist.

Name the largest species of mouse.
  A hippopotamouse.

If a straight line is the shortest distance
between two points, is a bee line the shortest
distance between two buzz stops?

The first apiary was started by a man who
liked to keep buzzy.

What do you call two pigs who live together?
  Pen pals.

*What would you do if an elephant sat in front
of you at a football match?*
  Miss most of the match.

Why do elephants have flat feet?
From jumping out of tall trees!

What do you get if an elephant sneezes?
  Out of the way!

What happened to Ray when he accidentally stepped on a lion?
  He became an X-Ray.

Why was the young kangaroo thrown out by his mother?
  For smoking in bed!

What are frogs' favourite tales?
  Croak and dagger stories.

Where do tadpoles change into frogs?
  In the croakroom.

What's tall and smells nice?
  A graff-odil.

What do you get if you cross a giraffe and a hedgehog?
  An eight-foot tall toothbrush!

Why do giraffes have such long necks?
  So they don't have to smell their feet!

OFFENSIVE EFFLUVIA!

Customer: Bring me a dragon sandwich.
Waiter: Sorry, sir — we've run out of bread.

You can never joke with a snake — you can't pull its leg!

What's a snake's favourite food?
Hiss Fingers.

What did the mouse say when it chipped its front teeth?
Hard cheese.

Why is a horse like a cricket match?
Because it gets stopped by the rein.

Where do parrots go with three A-levels?
    A pollytechnic.

What do geese watch on TV?
    Duckumentaries.

What's the best year for kangaroos?
    Leap year.

How do you catch a squirrel?
    Climb up a tree and act like a nut!

What did the stag say to his children?
  Hurry up, deers.

What do you call high-rise flats for pigs?
  Sty scrapers.

Why is a pig in a kitchen like a house on fire?
  The sooner you put it out the better!

What did the pig say when the farmer grabbed him by the tail?
  This is the end of me!

Where do beavers keep their savings?
In the river bank.

What happened to the piglet who wanted to be in a Shakespeare play?
He ended up as HAMlet.

Cross a sheep with a kangaroo and what do you get?
A jumper with a pocket.

What are assets?
   Little donkeys.

How does a sheep keep warm in winter?
   Central bleating.

Why does a rabbit have a shiny nose?
   Because its powder puff is at the other end.

Where do tadpoles go when they lose their tails?
   To a retail shop.

What do we call a frog who's a spy?
   A croak-and-dagger agent.

Cross a frog with a can of cola and you wind up with a new beverage — a croak-a-cola!

How can you tell which end of a worm is his head?
Tickle his middle and see which end smiles!

Caterpillar — a worm in a fur coat.

Why do bees have sticky hair?
  Because they have honey combs.

What's worse than being a fool?
  Fooling with a bee.

Why couldn't the butterfly get into the dance?
  Because it was a moth-ball.

Where do jungle animals eat?
  At a beastro.

How does a photographer get a mouse to smile for a photograph?
  He tells the mouse, 'Say cheese.'

What do you call a duck that's a physician?
  A real quack.

'How do you make a statue of a gorilla?'
  'First you get a large piece of marble —
then you carve away everything that doesn't
look like a gorilla.'

*Cross a caretaker with an elephant and what do
you get?*
  A ten-ton corridor sweeper.

What do you get if you cross an elephant with a boy scout?

An elephant that helps old ladies across the road.

What did the elephant singer say into the microphone?
Tusking — one, two, three — tusking . . .

Did you hear about the elephant who went away to forget?

Why do elephants eat so many peanuts?
Because people don't offer them anything else!

There's a sign in a safari park which reads:
TRESPASSERS WILL BE EATEN!

First girl: That butterfly used to be a caterpillar.
Friend: I knew it looked familiar!

One kid asked his parents, 'If fish are always in water, why don't they get rusty?'

'My brother swallowed a frog.'
'Did it make him sick?'
'He's liable to croak any minute!'

Baby snake: Am I poisonous?
Mother: Why do you ask?
Baby snake: Because I've just bitten my lip!

A man was complaining to a pet shop owner, 'Six months ago I bought two rabbits, put them together in the same cage, and I still have only two rabbits.'

The owner explained, 'There's a perfectly good reason — they're both brothers!'

'You're late,' said one frog to another.
'I know — I got stuck in somebody's throat.'

Teacher: What's a panther?
Little girl: That's a man who makes pants.

Turtles have good memories — in fact, they have turtle recall!

Most rabbits have had lots of hare-raising experiences.

One seabird to another:
  'I tell you, you're just too gullible.'

Two reindeer were talking. One asked the other, 'How was the stag party?'

One donkey asked another, 'But if you don't believe in God, who do you bray to?'

Mama Bear to Papa Bear, 'Wake up — it's half past April!'

One camel to another 'I don't care what people say — I'm thirsty!'

Mickey Mouse is in an gnaw-ful mood!

Baby Penguin: Are you sure I'm a penguin?
Mama Penguin: Why do you ask?
Baby Penguin: Because I'm freezing!

A sweating snail was following a turtle. He yelled out, 'I wish you would stop rushing!'

Woodpeckers — birds that talk through morse code.

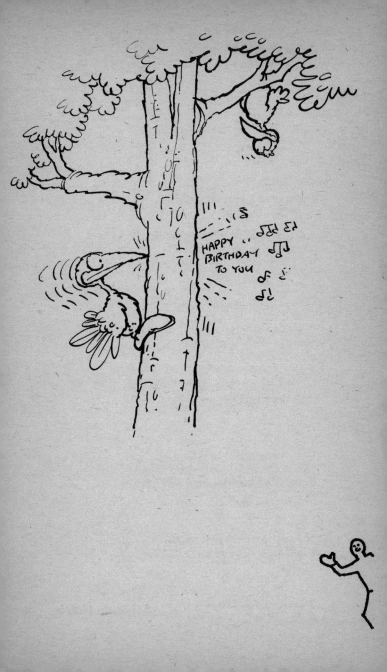

A female pig told her husband, 'You're beginning to *boar* me!'

A pig that investigates murders is a member of the *Hamicide* Squad.

First kangaroo: Where's your baby?
Second kangaroo: My goodness — my pocket has been picked!

Squirrels are like some people — they worry too much about nuttin'!

Mother skunk to child: 'Children should be smelled — not heard.'

First Pig: How's your food?
Second Pig: It tastes *swill*!

Did you hear about the two rabbits that got married and went on a bunnymoon?

First goat: Who's that little goat.
Second goat: That's my kid brother.

A baby rabbit kept pestering its mother. 'Where did I come from, Mom? Huh? Huh? Where did I come from?'

The baby rabbit nagged until its mother finally said, 'Stop bothering me, Junior. If you must know, you were pulled out of a magician's hat.'

MA MA!

One snake sang to another, 'Give me a little hiss, will 'ya hon . . .'

'Is it true that carrots improve your sight?'
'Have you ever seen a rabbit with glasses?'

'It takes three sheep to make just one sweater.'
    'I didn't even know that sheep could knit!'

Lem: Did you hear about the turtle on the motorway?
Clem: What was the turtle doing on the motorway?
Lem: About one mile an hour.

Two skunks were talking about their existence.
First skunk: But, René — how can you be certain you really exist?
Second skunk: I stink, therefore I am.

Is a pig who parks cars a porking lot attendant?

One pig actor was annoyed at another pig actor because he kept hogging the stage!

Baby rabbit: How much is 6,229 times 5,672?
Mama rabbit: I can't do sums that so fast.
Baby rabbit: Then why do they say that rabbits multiply quickly?

Rabbits can multiply, but only a snake can be an adder.

'Why do you call your dog Camera?'
    'Because he's always snapping.'

'My brother does bird impressions.'
    'Really?'
    'Yes — he eats worms!'

'I met a farmer who's a magician.'
    'How do you know?'
    'He told me he was going to turn his cow into a field.'

'Why does an ostrich have such a long neck?'
    'It has to — after all, it's heads is very far away from its body.'

Old lady: You shouldn't pull faces at that bull-dog.
Young girl: But he started it!

'Did you ever see a man-eating tiger?
  'No, but I've seen a man eating chicken.'

Newsflash: Fifty dogs have been stolen from a kennel. Police claim they have no leads.

'In the park I was surrounded by lions.'
  'Lions in the park?'
  'That's right — dandelions!'

Customer: You sold me this canary yesterday and I discovered it was lame.
Salesman: What do you want — a singer or a dancer?